ACKNOWLEDGMENTS

This historically oriented work is a product of my education, which stressed the need for understanding the root cause of significant ideas and events. Here, the cause of any philosopher's thought often lies in his life and times. I would like to thank my graduate and undergraduate schools for some of the ideas contained in this work—and this includes many teachers at both St. John's and St. Joseph's University: Dr. Sebastian Matczak, Dr. Anna-Teresa Tymieniecka, Dr. James Byrne, Dr. Augustin Riska, Frs. Hogan and Browne of St. John's; Dr. David Marshall, Drs. Linehan, Godfrey and Jenemann and Dr. Larry McKinnon in Philosophy at St. Joseph's, and also Dr. Francis Olley in the English Department, Dr. David Burton in History, and Mr. Kipphorn in Modern Foreign Languages, also in St. Joseph's.

The administration, faculty and students at Holy Family College, Torresdale, Pennsylvania have always been extremely cooperative—particularly its president, Sr. Francesca Onley, Dr. Lisa Woodside, Dean of the College, Dr. Schiavo, Assistant Dean, Dr. Catherine Moyer, Division Head in Liberal Arts and Sciences, Dr. Patricia Michael, Chairman in Humanities, Drs. Arthur Grugan and Regina Hobaugh in Philosophy, and Dr. Thomas McCormack. Finally, much gratitude to my mother and uncle.

The outstanding typesetting is the work of Mr. Thomas Mau of the 69th Street Terminal Press, Upper Darby, PA.

FIVE

PLAYS

UNIVERSITY
PRESS OF
AMERICA

Lanham • New York • London

Copyright © 1992 by
University Press of America®, Inc.
4720 Boston Way
Lanham, Maryland 20706

3 Henrietta Street
London WC2E 8LU England

Library of Congress Cataloging-in-Publication Data

Settanni, Harry, 1945–
Five philosophers : how their lives influenced their thought / by
Harry Settanni.
p.   cm.
1. Philosophers—Biography.   2. Philosophers—Psychology.
3. Philosophy—Psychological aspects.   I. Title.
B104.S45   1992   190—dc20   92–7912 CIP
[B]

ISBN 0–8191–8636–8 (alk. paper)

 The paper used in this publication meets the minimum requirements of
American National Standard for Information Sciences—Permanence
of Paper for Printed Library Materials, ANSI Z39.48–1984.

FIVE PHILOSOPHERS

CONTENTS

FIVE PHILOSOPHERS

INTRODUCTION

There is probably an old saying that no philosopher has philosophized in a vacuum. Quite to the contrary, most philosophies listed in the history of philosophy are, to at least some extent, a product of their times and of the life of the philosopher. This is the theme which I would like to explore throughout this work; namely, the impact of the philosopher's life and times upon his philosophical ideas. I will attempt to elaborate a thesis that, very often, a philosophy or philosophical system is the result of a philosopher's attempt to synthetize or possibly just to reconcile an underlying dualism. That dualism or duality will constitute a problem for a philosopher — a problem he tries to solve, sometimes by synthesis. The source of that duality may spring from any source in the philosopher's life and/or times. For example, there may be an underlying opposition between the philosopher's life or upbringing and his times, and this will constitute a duality. Or, in other cases, a duality may arise from two very opposed or simply different social or political movements in the time or century in which the philosopher lived. Finally, the duality may appear as a result of different influences in the philosopher's upbringing. All these combinations are possible, and I intend to explore all possible combinations.

It is true that one cannot hold to the claim that all philosophies are necessarily the product mainly of a philosopher's life and times but many, perhaps most philosophical systems, are related to their environment in this manner. Philosophical systems are not skeletons; they have flesh and blood, and they relate to the world around them. In recent years, this has become almost a truism.

For our immediate purposes, we will examine the life and times of five philosophers who were prominent in history: John Stuart Mill, Immanuel Kant, Georg Wilhelm Friedrich Hegel, John Dewey, and Immanual Mounier.

The name of John Stuart Mill, with whom we will begin, is prominent in Anglo-American Philosophy. The English Empirical School of Philosophy and Psychology dominated many of his writings, especially his masterpiece in the history of philosophy, The Principles of Logic. Here, Mill elaborated his famous Theory of Induction in philosophy and also attempted to formulate the logical basis of social theory. Empiricism and Logic formed one strain in Mill's thinking and the interest in both social issues and social theory formed the other. The interest in social theory, the latter interest, was expressed in several writings which will be mentioned later, but probably found its most perfect and most famous expression in Mill's treatise On Liberty. An interest in Logic, on the one hand, and an interest in the problems of society on the other; i.e., an interest, again, in social issues and social theory. Why these seemingly divergent interests on the part of this Anglo-American philosopher? Did the two strains in his thought, Logic, and Social Theory and Issues ever harmonize?

INTRODUCTION

The first chapter, "J. S. Mill: The Influence of Father and Wife", will attempt to deal with the problem of this underlying duality in all of Mill's thinking and writing. What influences were at work here? In Mill's case, we can find many external forces at work in the formation of both Mill's Logic and interest in society operative in the nineteenth century, Mill's era. But perhaps even more interesting than the era in which he lived are the external forces and influences operative in Mill's life. A great deal of care and time will be taken in elaborating just these influences.

The education of J. S. Mill under the single tutelage of his father, James, has become famous in the history of philosophy. James Mill exerted a preeminent influence on the thinking of one of the great philosophers in history, and it is this formative influence of his father in the thinking of J. S. Mill which will be traced in the first chapter. It will be shown here how James Mill, in his private household and exercising this private form of education, molded the mind of his son, John Stuart, in the direction of a bent and proclivity toward logic. In logic, John Stuart revealed himself to be truly a child prodigy.

However, especially in later life, logic was not the only direction which the mind of J. S. Mill later took. There was also the influence of Harriett Taylor Mill who later became his wife. Harriett Taylor was an intelligent woman who was interested in social reform. Mill adapted these more concrete interests in later life as he became disenchanted with purely logical schemes for reforming the world, such as those found present in, for example, Utilitarianism. It was to the later period in Mill's life that many of his famous works on social reform, beginning with On Liberty, were written. It was also in later life that Mill began to exhibit an interest in Socialism, whether or not he ever later actually became a Socialist.

In the biography of J. S. Mill, it appears that there were two powerful formative influences, father and wife, or James Mill and Harriett Taylor Mill. In later life, Mill rebelled, at least to some degree, against the sternness of his father's upbringing in Logic and the Classics, and, after a brief period of mental breakdown, discovered that there was more to life than pure logic. It was here that he met Harriett, and it was she who changed his life in the direction of a more concrete concern with human society.

Did Mill ever synthetize these divergent interests, the almost dualistic influence of father and wife? Such a unification often appears to have been the central problem of his life and some unification of interests appears when Mill attempts to create a logic of the sciences in his A System of Logic: Ratiocinative and Inductive. But it also appears that, in other respects, the mutually opposing influences of father and wife are not so easily synthetized as exhibited, for example, in the great difference in style and content between the Principles of Logic and On Liberty. At any rate, the completed philosophy of J. S. Mill often appears to represent a fundamental tension between different, possibly opposing interests, abstract logic and concrete social concern, or the influence of father and wife. In Chapter One, it will be explained in much detail how both of these factors in Mill's life heavily influenced his philosophy.

But Mill was not the only philosopher who exhibited a fundamental duality awaiting a synthesis as the fundamental problem and driving force of his philosophy. The same underlying duality and tension was present in the life and writing of another extremely prominent philosopher in the Western World, Immanuel Kant. The key to much of Immanual Kant's philosophy lies in a fundamental tension between his Pietistic, religious upbringing and the Age of Reason or the "Aufklarung" of the eighteenth century in which he lived. Kant's problem was the problem of somehow making harmonious the scientific philosophy of his age with religion. There was a central conflict in much of the eighteenth century Enlightenment concerning man. Did man have free choice or was he merely a machine? According to some of the "philosophies" of the Age of Reason such as La Mettrie, if we really studied man scientifically, we would know that he was really a machine and that the human body followed the laws of the machine. La Mettrie compared the human being to a statue in his famous work, Man, the Machine.

But, according to all the established religions, then as now, man had free choice. He could freely decide between good and evil, to directing his life towards salvation or towards damnation. If he freely chose the good life, he would be rewarded in heaven; if he chose the evil life, he would be punished in hell. On the other hand, if, as thinkers such as La Mettrie claimed, man were merely a machine, then the act of praising or blaming an individual for anything would not make much sense. The machine, after all, cannot choose either to work or to take it easy on a given day.

How could one make sense of morality unless it was based on free choice? But according to some views of science prevalent at the time, man had no more free choice than a machine. Could religion and science be reconciled? Kant thought that it could and his attempt at synthesis between science and religion, although not the first of such attempts nor the last, was very original. And it is Kant's attempt at such a synthesis between his Christian-based ethics and his scientifically-based metaphysics which constitutes the core of the second chapter, "Immanual Kant: The Rift Between Religion and Science". In the same chapter, I will also explore the possible origins of the Kantian concepts, "noumena" and "phenomena" or of things-in-themselves and things-as-they-appear to us. In the realm of things-as-they-appear to us, man operates according to scientific causal laws, very much like the behavior of La Mettrie's machine; but in the realm of things-in-themselves or noumena, man is free.

A very similar problem concerning the inherent duality of things and a similarly pressing attempt to solve the problem appeared to present itself to Hegel in the very early nineteenth century, around the time of the death of Kant. In Hegel's case, the problem was primarily a political duality which was present in the early nineteenth century, a duality between the concept of Freedom as expressed in French Revolution, which Hegel called "negative freedom" in his <u>Phenomenology of Mind</u> and the need for national unification of his native Germany which was divided into three hundred small, often warring principalities.

Now in Hegel's time, there was plainly a need for both; both "unification" and freedom for the individual. Of all philosophers, Hegel was certainly a product of his times. Hegelian metaphysics is certainly a time-bound, Process Philosophy. The urgent problem for Hegel is one which beset all of his philosophy; namely, how to make syntheses out of opposing tendencies, but especially of opposing political tendencies. Many commentators of Hegel have viewed his entire philosophy as arising from a great need to solve urgent political, social problems.

And, indeed, Hegel thought he solved the political problem of his day; namely, the problem of reconciling the freedom of the individual with the need for political solidarity in the synthesis known as "positive freedom". Hegel's problem will be dealt with in Chapter Three on "G.W.F. Hegel: The Surrounding Political World". In Hegel, we have a philosopher who was certainly affected by the times in which he lived.

Finally, we move to two philosophers of the twentieth century, John Dewey and Emmanuel Mounier; and here, once again, understanding the life and times in which the philosopher lived becomes vital to the understanding of the thought of the individual philosopher. Chapter Four will deal with John Dewey, a very progressive thinker in our own century, who responded very sensitively to more recent currents of thought in both the areas of science and of democratic politics. These underlying, somewhat divergent streams in the world of the twentieth century, constituted not so much problems for John Dewey as they constituted solutions to political and philosophical problems in the time of the twentieth century. For all these reasons, I have called the Fourth Chapter, "John Dewey and the Twentieth Century".

In the last chapter, we will take a look at a less well-known philosopher, the probable founder of the small but significant contemporary philosophy known as Personalism. It was Emmanuel Mounier who thought that personal relationships were more important than the conquest of nature or the acquisition of money. The person and his problems, according to Mounier, should be placed at the center of philosophy and it was impossible to philosophize without him. The Existentialists may well have been influenced by the Personalist stream of thought. Certainly, both of these philosophies closely resemble one another. Both philosophies, in turn, were affected by the era or times in which they were created.

What is true of Hegel is almost as true of Mounier. He was certainly a product of his time. For Mounier, as may also be true, in a limited extent, in our own time, the respective ideologies of Capitalism and Communism competed aggressively for the minds of men and women everywhere. Who was right? This was the most pressing problem in the era of Mounier, which corresponds roughly, at least in the closing years of his life, with the years of the international Cold War. Even today, this is still something of a problem.

In the chapter, "Emmanuel Mounier: Capitalism and Communism", I will detail Mounier's struggle to find a synthesis between the inhumanity of Communist tyranny and the inhumanity of Capitalism gone wild. He calls this synthesis the philosophy of Personalism, a philosophy in which the true dignity of the human person is at the center of everything. It was a synthesis framed in the world of the twentieth century. Mounier worked, in this context, toward the solution of very concrete, practical problems. I will describe these also in the last chapter.

It is my fond hope that this small contribution will add to the growing conviction on the part of many that philosophy exists in a specific context, that it does not grow out of a vacuum, and that the flesh and blood of philosophy itself is comprised of the concrete life and unique historical time of the philosopher from which it originated, and after which it even went on to influence that unique historical time and possibly even other historical times after that.

Let us proceed to our history, beginning with the unusual life and times of John Stuart Mill.

CHAPTER ONE

J. S. MILL: THE INFLUENCE OF FATHER AND WIFE

John Stuart Mill was the product of two powerful forces operative in his life; the underlying influence of his father and the underlying, almost secret influence, of his wife. In addition, like almost every other philosopher, Mill was the product of his times. In this chapter, I wish to explore, as much as possible, the range of each of these influences upon the philosophy of John Stuart Mill, especially the mutually enforcing influences of father and wife.

Not that these were necessarily influences moving in the same direction. To the contrary, the influence of both James Mill and Harriett Taylor could be described, even, as antagonistic influences. But it is precisely this antagonism, this dualism, that J. S. Mill attempted to resolve throughout his entire philosophy.

A. The Nineteenth Century

Even before we enter upon an analysis of the influence of father and wife in the life of J. S. Mill, it might be a good idea to explore some of the fundamental currents of thought working within the nineteenth century, the century in which Mill lived, and of which both he and most of the other intellectuals of his century were well aware.

1. Classicism vs. Romanticism

In listing influences upon the life and thought of Mill, let us mention first of all that favorite of all nineteenth century oppositions — the opposition between Classicism and Romanticism. Mill writes about this opposition at some length in his Autobiography. They seemed to Mill to resemble very much the two edges of a sword. On one edge of the sword stood all the Classical values; on the other edge stood all the values of the Romantic world.[1]

a. Values of Classicism

The Classical values were celebrated by many authors and critics of the eighteenth century, an example of whom would be the famous eighteenth century poet, Alexander Pope. The Classicist in literature, in many respects like Pope himself, celebrated structure and form and following the rules over the values of content; the eternal to the historical, and the metaphysical to the concrete. Classicism was the original home of John Stuart Mill in the sense that this was the training which he received from his father, James.

James Mill was a scholarly man who earned his living as a journalist. But he was primarily imbued with the spirit of the Classics and it was Attic Greek and the Classics which he taught to all of his eight children, including his son, John Stuart. In addition, all of James' children received extensive training in logic. It was this stress upon logic from which John Stuart claimed he had learned the most.[2] And logic, in many ways, formed the backbone of the Classical view of the world with its emphasis upon the correct form. In a similar manner, logic has only one correct answer, and this answer will be arrived at if the correct form is followed.

Another element inherent in the Classical view of the world is often an insistence on a scientific view of the world; again, an insistence on the value of following the correct form, of following the right rules; here, the rules of inductive logic. In the history of philosophy, Mill is famous for, among other things, his formulation of the Rules of Inductive Logic. The five canons of Induction of John Stuart Mill are well known today.

It was primarily in formulating the Principles of Logic, a well-known work of John Stuart Mill, that he reveals his debt to the Classical view of the world. The Classical world-view was formulated in eighteenth century literature but it was a world-view developed, elaborated and argued for throughout nineteenth century literature, as one side of the two-edged sword, with Romanticism on the other side.

The J. S. Mill of the Principles of Logic was, above all else, a Classicist, pursuing what he thought was the correct scientific method and concurring with the Classical view that there was a correct method or proper form in every subject matter. It was this same Classical view of the world which never completely left Mill, even in his later writings. Hence, even in his later political and economic writings, there is still the same insistence on the logical, scientific view of the world.

But John Stuart's Classical upbringing and his hankering after the Classical ideal of logic, although never completely abandoned, was later modified. The later writings of Mill, particularly the political-economic writings, together with the posthumous Essays on Theism are no longer bounded or circumscribed by the classic, logical view of the world. For the later Mill, there was more to life than sheer logic.

And it was in this later tendency that we begin to see John Stuart's ability to amalgamate and assimilate many of the central tenets and creeds of Classicism's seeming opposite in the nineteenth century, namely Romanticism. It is here that Mill begins to understand that life is more than correct form, more than mere definitions. Life includes the role of feelings, and it is feelings which the movement of Romanticism in literature and, for that matter, in painting and in music, concerned itself.

b. Values of Romanticism

Romanticism, according to Mill, comprised the other edge of the two-edged sword. Again, it was the Romanticist, in Mill's analysis, who praised the values of content over form, of the historical over the eternal, of the concrete over the metaphysical. It was to this rich world full of concrete content and a sense of the historical that Mill was brought by many events in his events in his life; most notably, the death of both his father and his wife.

First of all, with his father's death, Mill felt a sense of independence which he had never felt before. All of this, he records in his Autobiography, in the form of a dream premonition, which he had while his father was still alive.[3] In the dream, he was told that his father had died and that he would now have to take over all the affairs of the household with his family of eight, including sisters and brothers.

In real life, at the later point of his father's death, Mill actually began to diverge from his father's opinions in politics, which his father wrote in the Analysis of the Phenomena of the Mind. In politics, he began to see the actual value of Socialism in economic reform, which values were more or less anathema to James Mill and all of the early Utilitarians.

Also, Mill's marriage to and the later death of his wife, Harriett, added to his overall sense that there was more to life than logic. And it was this later tragic sense of life that emerges in the political-economic writings such as On Liberty, but most especially, in the posthumous essays, Three Essays on Theism, and also in Socialism.[3]

It is here that John Stuart Mill, plainly in line with a more Romantic view of life, begins to prefer the historical over the eternal; the concrete to the metaphysical; and the value of content over that of merely following the logical rules. It is here that Mill begins to be imbued with the tragic sense of life.

Nevertheless, as already mentioned, the sense of the Classical values never leaves him even if, to a certain extent, the Classical view of the world does leave him. Mill never embraced the Romantic worldview wholeheartedly as he never really embraced the worldview of the Classicists. But out of both of these seemingly opposite conceptions of the world Mill would make his own amalgam or compromise.

It cannot really be said that Mill ever made a synthesis out of these contrasting movements. But perhaps, if he could not really make a synthesis in his mature philosophy with which we will shortly be dealing, or if no synthesis were possible, then he certainly attempted to make the best he could out of the more positive characteristics of each of these worldviews.

2. Mill's Assessment

For Mill, it was obviously a question of which side of the two-edged sword to adopt. But both sides looked promising if looked upon objectively.

a. Autobiography

In the Autobiography, it came down to the question of why it would be necessary to throw out anything on either side if anything appeared to be salvageable. And for Mill, almost everything was salvageable as long as it did not run to extremes. Both the eternal and the historical were needed; both the concrete and abstract; both form and content.

Plainly, for Mill, as well as for others, it was impossible to have one at the expense of the other. The eternal and the historical went together; so did the concrete and the abstract; and the same was true of form and content; they went together. No one could divorce one element from the other.

The eternal divorced from the historical was senseless; so was the historical sense divorced from the sense of the eternal and, likewise, with the others. No dichotomy could, in the long run, make any sense. The concrete could not be divorced from the abstract any more than the abstract could be divorced from the concrete. And similarly, it would be just as impossible to separate content from form as it would be impossible to separate form from content.

So why all of this bickering between the Classic and Romantic currents of thought in the nineteenth century? The mood of compromise between these two frequently quarreling modes of thought best suited J. S. Mill's mentality. And it is this mentality which has given to the world such works as A System of Logic: Ratiocinative and Inductive and also On Liberty and On the Subjection of Women, which will be the topic of analysis in this chapter.

In these works, Mill plainly reveals the almost dualistic Spirit of the Age of which he was a part Classicism, on the one hand, in the more logical works, and Romanticism, on the other, primarily in the later political works. The writings and the philosophy of John Stuart Mill, like the age of which it was a part, reveal the impact of the warring philosophies or worldviews of Classicism and Romanticism.

b. Impact on His Thought

It was from the Classical worldview that J. S. Mill adapted his sense of logic and his belief in the necessity of social reform; however, it was from the Romantic worldview that Mill learned the value of feelings, both for their own sake in the formation of a human being and, also, as an instrument in understanding our natural solidarity with every other human being who has ever existed. The impact of the Romantic worldview may be somewhat evident in On Liberty, but it is even more evident in such posthumous works as Socialism and Three Essays on Theism.

It is evident that the two-edged sword of the times affected Mill's thought. These outer circles of Romanticism and Classicism were definitely present. But one might also claim that in the same way more inner circles were also present as influences on the life and thought of our John Stuart.

Paralleling these outer spheres in many ways were the mutual or, rather, mutually antagonistic circles of father and wife. Both of these exerted an influence, a force in the life of John Stuart as we have already seen. We might claim that influence of James Mill is a Classical influence and that the influence of Harriett Taylor is a Romantic influence, although this would be somewhat simplifying matters.

At any rate, it will be shown that the inner circles do roughly correspond to the outer circles in this matter. In other words, one might consider the mutually antagonistic influences of father and wife as concentric circles.

We have already explored the outer spheres of these concentric circles. It is to the inner spheres, the spheres of father and wife, to which we will now turn. How did these spheres influence the life and thought of Mill? Let us view this in more detail.

B. James Mill and Logic

According to J. S. Mill, what he learned most from his father was logic. Many people who were otherwise educated did not know how to argue logically, in Mill's opinion. When they attempted to refute an argument, they would begin an entirely new argument on completely different foundations without ever refuting the old argument. By doing this, they left both arguments as equal in strength. Their strategy plainly revealed a lack of training in logic.

1. Classic Values in Autobiography

James Mill was a journalist who admired all of the classic values embodied in ancient Greece. He taught all of his eight children Attic Greek, and he also drilled them in the logic of Aristotle. James Mill was born in Scotland, the son of a shoemaker. The class structure in his time was such that he could not rise nearly as high as his talents might take him. He applied for the ministry but was never granted a parish. This was both because he never mastered any of the local Scottish dialects and also because doubts about the existence of God began to visit him./

How, he wondered, could an all-good God allow all of the misery which took place in the world to happen? Why were some men, like James Mill, born poor and rendered incapable of rising very far above their station?

He eventually settled down in a London ghetto and became a journalist, championing the cause of the poor and of social reform. He joined a small group, which included Jeremy Bentham, and which called itself collectively the Philosophic Radicals.

While working on his journalism and also on the book which was to make him famous, a History of British India, James Mill yet found time to teach his children. He refused to send them to any of the public schools of the day or to a university since this would stultify any natural genius they might possess. Writing away at his desk, he used flash cards to teach his children. John Stuart was often appointed the task of teaching the others, which he hated.

There was one defect in his education which Mill records in his Autobiography. Whenever he asked his father about the meaning of anything, his father would always give a definition instead of an example. Mill claimed he grew up knowing the abstract definition of everything, but he was never familiar with a single concrete reality.[5]

This method of education, which John Stuart received under his father, James, was satirized by Charles Dickens in his novel, Hard Times. Gradgrind is the schoolmaster in this novel and one small boy, whom he teaches, asks him what a horse is. Gradgrind tells him that a horse is "an equiline quadraped which feeds upon ——". Then his wife, Sissy Jupe, in the novel, shows the small boy a picture. "This is a horse", she tells him.

b. Deduction in Principles of Psychology

The deductive method figures prominently in James Mill's Principles of Psychology. His analysis of the mind works on the principle of association of the idea with another. It also proceeds according to deduction, advancing from the general to the less general. This is basically the method of definition.

2. J. S. Mill's A System of Logic

The System of Logic: Ratiocinative and Inductive published in 1843 is Mill's masterpiece. It represents the culmination of his early upbringing and training in logic under his father. But it also represents the beginnings of John Stuart's breakaway to independent patterns and habits of thought. The book describes both inductive and deductive logic and, finally, their combination in the so-called "inverse deductive" method.

a. Tribute to Deductive Logic

John Stuart Mill never completely broke away from the deductive method of his father. In his logic in 1843, he found room for it.[6] In the nineteenth century world of J. S. Mill, another debate was brewing besides the one concerned with Classicism and Romanticism. It was the debate over the relative e merits of the deductive method and the inductive method in logic.

Deduction proceeds from the general to the less general, whereas induction proceeds in the opposite direction. It moves from the particular to the less particular. An example of deduction would be the famous example:

> All men are mortal
>
> Socrates is a man
>
> Therefore, Socrates is mortal.

This is also the method of definition: first, describe the more general, then the less general class. For example, man is an animal who is rational. An example of induction would be:

> The first swan I saw was white.
>
> The second swan I saw was white.
>
> The third swan I saw was white.
>
> Therefore, all swans are white.

We can never know this, however, with certainty, only that the conclusion to this inference is probable. Although it is unlikely, we may always meet a white swan.

For some in the nineteenth century, only induction provided the path to new knowledge and made genuine discoveries, genuine additions to our store of knowledge. For its critics, deduction could not accomplish the same feat. It could never add to our store of knowledge. It was simply a compendium of knowledge which already existed. The deductive method could easily be dispensed with; induction, never.

J. S. Mill disagreed. Or rather, he agreed that deduction could never establish new knowledge; but the function of deduction was, rather, the conservative one of insuring consistency in the knowledge which we already possessed.

In conjunction with induction, through which new knowledge was established, it served a useful purpose. It is in his defense of a limited role for deduction that J. S. Mill reveals himself to be, in some ways, still under the sway of his thought, an influence which he never abandoned entirely, though he modified its direction.

b. Discovery of Inductive Logic

It was in his employment of the inductive method that Mill was a trailblazer. In this new method he excelled; and, in the history of philosophy, Mill's name is famous for the Five Canons of Rules of Induction. Collectively, these methods establish what are the necessary conditions in any particular instance for an inference to take place and be correct. This, in turn, will depend upon the degree of resemblance in the sample.

Mill claimed that induction worked only because there was some general uniformity throughout Nature.[7] But how do we know that Nature is uniform?[8] This seems to lead into a vicious circle. How can we prove the Uniformity of Nature?

This became a problem shortly after Mill published the Logic and it remains a problem today. We know that induction, more often than not, works. Why does it work? It appears that we can only justify induction on pragmatic grounds; i.e., the grounds of the possible consequences. Here we could state that if, and only if, Nature is uniform, will induction work. Induction works so Nature must be uniform throughout.

Induction remains a problem. Some today attempt to justify it on the grounds of probability or on pragmatic grounds. But Mill's attempt to ground induction in the Uniformity of Nature remains, even today, a pioneering attempt despite all the problems that surround it. It was in his use of the inductive method that Mill strikes out more clearly on his own, and the Classic influence of his father is less discernible.

c. Applications in Sociology

But could logic ever be applied to sociology and the problems of social reform? Mill thought that it could. His attempt to apply it here culminated in what he called the "Inverse Deductive" Method. This amounts to a combination of the inductive method with the deductive method. One begins inductively with particular samples and then generalizes to laws. These laws, in turn, then could be applied deductively to less general phenomena.

This may not be exactly Romanticism, but it is plainly, also, no simple deductive logic here - no simple Greek Classicism inherited from his father. Here again, Mill moves out on his own, farther and farther away from his father's orbit, and becomes once again something of a trailblazer.

C. Harriett Taylor Mill and Socialism

Harriett Taylor was an intelligent woman who was interested in social reform and in Socialism. Mill met her in 1841, just before the publication of his major work, the Logic, while his father was still living. At the time, she was a married woman. Despite the fact that his father seemed to frown upon it, Mill courted her. After her husband died in 1850, Mill married her. When she, in turn, died in 1859, Mill wrote that he felt as though the wellspring of his life had been broken. Every year of his life thereafter he spent half the year in Avignon, France, by her graveside.[9]

1. Her Interest in Social Reform

Harriett's interest in the problems of society had a concrete influence on John Stuart Mill, an influence in the direction of the heart. It is now years after Mill's mental crisis of 1826 which he recorded in his autobiography. From his father, he had learned an abstract interest in the problems of social reform; but through Harriett, his interest in social reform is now concrete; not an interest filled solely with Utilitarian theory and deductive logic.

a. Influence on Mill's Logic

We might surmise that Harriett Mill had some influence on the final stages of the compilation of Mill's enormous work, the Principles of Logic. The final books of the Logic deal squarely with the problem of finding a method for application in sociology and social reform, definitely Harriett Mill's sphere of interest.

Could their interests have overlapped here in the invention of this complex "Inverse Deductive Method"? Such a possibility is certainly more than remote for we find in the last three books of the Logic a method which is far from simple and which, as has already been mentioned, could not have been taken over from the spirit of Classical logic or from the spirit of Mill's Deduction.

b. Influence on His Politics

Certainly, the influence of Harriett Mill on Mill's later politics was enormous. According to one commentator, Mill constantly fantasized about her and identified her with the Spirit of Classical Greece because she wore her hair in a Greek bob. After meeting Harriett, the interest of John Stuart now shifts from logic and abstract political Utilitarian codes, embodying the goal of "the greatest good for the greatest number" to a concrete interest in the individual.

To this period belong all of Mill's famous political writings: On Liberty (1859), Representative Democracy (1863), On the Subjection of Women (1869) and Socialism (1874), which appeared posthumously.

2. J. S. Mill's On Liberty

In the realm of political theory, it is the single work on which most of his fame now rests.

a. The Brainstorm

Mill claims, in his Autobiography, that he conceived the idea of On Liberty while descending from the steps of the Capitol. He thought of making it a short article, but Harriett suggested that he expand it into an entire essay.

On Liberty was a courageous work for its day. It claimed that the right of the individual to do whatever he pleased, no matter how odious that might be in the eyes of others, reigned supreme and that the State could not curtail this right under any pretext whatsoever except that of "clear and immediate danger of harm to others". This proviso, of course, left it to future generations to define "clear and immediate danger of harm to others"; but, for some, the cause of civil liberties already begun with John Stuart Mill was on the march.

b. The Role of Harriett Mill

Here, as elsewhere in his politics, Harriett Mill was committed to the central thesis of On Liberty, which amounts to a defense of the rights of the individual against the State. One cannot derive this defense of individual rights from J. S. Mill's earlier Utilitarian credo, "the greatest good for the greatest number". This may be a very democratic creed but it is also, in many ways, society oriented. The creed mentions the rights of the majority but nothing about the rights of an unpopular individual who might stand against the crowd.

Can one really defend the rights of the individual to free speech on the basis of the Utilitarian philosophy of "the greatest good for the greatest number"? This question is often debated today but one things is certain. That is, J. S. Mill did not derive the central tenet of On Liberty, which amounts to a defense of individual rights, from the earlier Utilitarian tenets of his father. Though Utilitarianism allowed ample room for the individual, it was basically a social creed and the defense of individual rights must lie elsewhere.

In all of his later political writings as well as in the Logic itself, J. S. Mill begins to break away from the simple Classic ideals of James Mill under the influence of Harriett Mill, a more Romantic influence. In later years, he plainly begins to prefer the concrete to the abstract, the historical to the metaphysical, and content to correct form. The life of J. S. Mill is simply one example in the history of philosophy of how a philosopher's life and times can influence his thought.

But there are many more examples. Let us now move to the case of Immanuel Kant in eighteenth century Germany for he is a living influence today.

[1] J. S. Mill, "Coleridge" in Dissertations and Discussions. (Collected Works, Vol.I)

[2] J. S. Mill, Autobiography, pp.13-14.

[3] Cf. A. W. Levy. "The Mental Crisis of John Stuart Mill", Psychoanalytic Review,   Vol.32(1945), pp.86-101.

[4] On the death of his wife, cf. L. Stephan, The English Utilitarians, Vol.III, p.56.

[5] M. J. Packe, The Life of John Stuart Mill, p.24.

[6] J. S. Mill, A System of Logic, Bk.II, Ch.III, Sec.7, pp.133-134.

[7] J. S. Mill, op.cit., Bk.II, Ch.III, Sec.2, pp.203-205.

[8] J. S. Mill, op.cit., Bk.III, Ch.III, Sec.3, p.205.

[9] Leslie Stephan, op.cit., Vol.III, p.56.

CHAPTER TWO

IMMANUEL KANT: THE RIFT BETWEEN RELIGION AND SCIENCE

Kant's philosophy was built as an attempt to answer one question: Why has science made progress in getting answers to questions whereas metaphysics, the very heart of philosophy, has not?[1] Science kept teaching us more and more about the natural world surrounding us, whereas philosophy is no closer to the answer to its questions about the nature of reality than it was in the time of the ancient Greeks. True, these questions may forever be unanswerable; but, nevertheless, we will never stop asking them. Science makes progress, whereas philosophy always appears to be at the beginning of things.

Could philosophy once again be put upon the same footing as science? This was Immanuel Kant's question in the eighteenth century. This was the question he pondered in one form or another throughout much of his life. In his sixty-fourth year, he published the first of his three Critiques, all of which were one attempt to answer the question of how to put philosophy on a scientific basis.

According to Kant, science made progress because it stayed within the bounds of reason. Philosophy, on the other hand, seemed to be always asking questions which were beyond the capacity of our natural, human reason to answer. The first task, then, according to Kant, was to find the natural boundaries of human reason and then to stay within those boundaries. The task for philosophy was to determine the limits of natural reason. This in itself was no easy task but, without determining these boundaries, philosophy could never claim that it was a science. In order to be a science, philosophy must first of all pose the question, "What Can I Know?".

In Kant's opinion, in the speculative order, it appeared we could know nothing beyond what science told us. This was the essential point of Kant's first critique, The Critique of Pure Reason, which was published in 1781.[2] Science dealt with objects which were located in space and in time, so the human mind must confine itself to phenomena which were located in space and in time. For Kant, the mind was not structured to adequately answer questions about the origin of space and time itself; whether God created the world at a definite time in the past or whether the world always existed; whether space itself is infinite or whether it has boundaries. The human mind must confine itself to its scientific limits. It was structured to deal with space and time, not with whatever may lie beyond space and time.[3]

Nevertheless, what are we to say about these eternal questions which refuse to go away? What about those questions which the mind constantly keeps asking? The mind will always ask whether God exists even if it cannot prove this scientifically. The mind will always ask about itself whether it is immortal, even if this can never be proven in the eyes of science. The mind will never cease asking whether it really has free choice to follow the moral law or whether it is really conditioned to follow the laws of instinct like an animal and so not free but determined.

As Kant viewed the human condition, the mind will always keep asking questions which it can never answer but which it will never stop asking since the questions are presented by the nature of the mind itself.[4] Hence, it will always ask itself questions about the nature of GOD, FREEDOM and IMMORTALITY.[5] But, at least as far as speculative reason is concerned, it will never be able to prove that God exists. In the first critique, The Critique of Pure Reason, Kant defined the limits of speculative reason as he saw those limits. Here, the mind could not know about the existence of God through Speculative Reason and; also, through Speculative Reason, it could not know whether or not the universe had a beginning or whether it always existed. Kant's first Critique was his attempt to answer the first of three questions which humans are prone to ask. The questions are:

WHAT CAN I KNOW?

WHAT CAN I HOPE FOR?

WHAT CAN I DO?

To begin with, we can only know what Speculative Reason tells us and the message is place: Stay within the boundaries of space and time; i.e., the physical world of science. Nevertheless, can we hope for anything more than this? Can we do anything beyond what science seems to dictate that we can do? To these questions, Kant answers in the affirmative and both the questions and the answers form the subject matter of the next two Critiques.

Kant's Critique of Practical Reason is occupied with the questions WHAT CAN I DO? and also WHAT CAN I HOPE FOR? We must begin, for Kant, with the immediate intuition we all have of our own freedom. We know within ourselves that we possess free choice even if science cannot prove this. Science for Kant, as he mentions in The Critique of Pure Reason, can only tell us about things as they appear to us and not about things as they are in themselves. In other words, science can only tell us about phenomena and never about noumena.

Science deals only with phenomena and will, for this reason, always present to us a picture of man as determined in all of his actions like a machine. A machine has no free choice; neither does man. But science deals with man only in the phenomenal order; science deals with man only within the realm of space and time. Science does not tell us about noumena or, in other words, science does not tell us what man really is in himself.

In the realm of noumena, or of things-in-themselves, man is free, according to Kant. He has free choice and, for this reason, he is free to choose right from wrong and the moral world exists for him in the realm of noumena. The existence of the moral law implies a lawgiver for there is no moral law without a lawgiver. For this reason, a Supreme Lawgiver, God himself, exists.[6]

The Supreme Lawgiver, however, cannot mete out justice and rectify all wrongs within the short passage of a single lifetime. Reward and punishment, at least to some extent, can only be dispensed if the soul survives death; i.e., if the soul is immortal.

So the answer to the question WHAT CAN I DO? is to follow the moral law and the answer to the question WHAT CAN I HOPE FOR? is immortal life with God as a reward for following the moral law.

In this manner, religion and science are reconciled. But the seeming opposition of both religion and science forms the core of Kant's life and philosophy. How and why this is so we now wish to explore in some detail.

A. The Pietistic Background

Let us begin with Kant's upbringing as a devout Pietist. Pietism was a religion prominent in northern Germany which stressed the simple life and man's direct contact with and experience of God. Ritual was not important in this religion; it stressed simplicity and passion. Direct experience and the moral life were central to this religion, nothing else, including ritual seemed to matter.

Pietism was a religion well suited in some ways to agrarian life, chiefly because of its emphasis on direct, simple and austere passion. Much of its following in northern Germany consisted of farmers. In many respects, Pietism was a religion of farmers. Fulfilling the moral law and doing one's duty were all-important. One did not so much, as a Pietist, prove the existence of God as feel his existence in immediate experience.

One can easily imagine what impact this upbringing might have on the philosopher, Kant; hence, the importance of following the moral law in Kant's philosophy. Also, the stress on intuition or immediate experience in religion; i.e., one could not prove the existence of God or the immortality of the soul; these were a matter of experience or of intuition.[7]

1. Revolt Against Scholasticism

Historically, Pietism arose as a Protestant sect somewhat over a century after the Reformation began. Pietists essentially wanted a return to a religion of the heart, to a religion of enthusiasm. They thought that the original spirit of the Protestant Reformation had grown cold.

They looked upon the Scholastic philosophy operative within Lutheran Protestantism at that time as an oppressive intellectual structure which made religion into a rather dry affair. Religion had to return to its roots.

Religion had to be on fire with the love of Christ and the love of simple morality. But both of these very important sources of religion appeared to fade into the background before the Protestant Scholastic tradition, which attempted to rationalize religion. In Protestant Scholasticism, one attempted to prove the existence of God. For Pietists, God's existence was a matter of experience.

Religion, in the view of the Pietists, must either return to its early sources in experience and enthusiasm, it must either be on fire with the love of God and of Christ, or it must lose itself as religion.[8]

Pietism was primarily a religion of feeling, which advocated a return to simpler modes of life. The Protestant sect of the Mennonites can trace its ancestry back to the Pietists. Also, the Amish sects in Pennsylvania and elsewhere trace their roots back to the Mennonites and, hence, back to the Pietists.

The Amish traditionally have opposed modern technology and live by simpler, older methods of farming. They also live by a philosophy of non-violence.

2. Jacob Spener

In the seventeenth century, Jacob Spener wrote the Pia Desideria or The Heart on Fire. This work marked the birth of the Pietist movement. The "heart on fire" with the love of Christ does not attempt to rationalize the Christian religion as Spener thought too many of the Protestant churches of his own time were doing.

Such rationalizing rendered many churches and parishes a dull and spiritless affair. Spener's Heart on Fire was a devotional tract which helped to inspire the Pietist revolt against dry Scholasticism and also to return religion to its origins before the origins would become completely eroded through the force of slow, steady bureaucratic management and rationalization.[9]

The Pietist revolt in the seventeenth century represents very well one important stage in the story of the development of all religions. All religions originate with fiery zeal for their founder, which enthusiasm and ardor cools after a while under bureaucratic pressure. In this stage, the religion itself demands what amounts to a revival movement of which there have been many in the history of religion.

Even if the religious establishment itself does not look forward to such a revival, it must take place or religion itself will begin to lose its followers. These, in turn, will either leave the religion or become increasingly more indifferent.

In moments such as these, a so-called revival movement will take place. The Great Awakening of Johnathan Edwards in eighteenth century America is probably history's greatest, best-known example of a revivalist movement. Perhaps the Pentecostalist and Charismatic movement, also in the United States, could be considered as yet another. And smaller revivalist movements in religion take place with great frequency. The Pietist Revolt against dry Scholasticism in the seventeenth century was another one of these eternally recurring moments in the history of religion.

Kant was a Pietist. This upbringing under a devout Pietist mother, whom he remembered into his eighties, had a decided effect on his moral philosophy. How did it affect his philosophy as a whole?

B. Age of Enlightenment

The century in which Kant lived most of his life, the eighteenth century, is frequently known as the Age of Reason, or the Age of Enlightenment. The reason for this appelation is certainly not that everyone, most people, or even the intellectuals of the period were wise or even necessarily intelligent. The reason is, rather, that the eighteenth century witnessed the triumph of science in the minds of many of the intellectuals of that age.

Science had accomplished wonders. These were not technological wonders for, two hundred years ago, science was still in its infancy. But, two hundred years ago, science had proven its points; it had proven that its view of Nature was essentially correct. It was proven that the earth moved around the sun; that the heart circulated blood through the body.

Science, in short, gave us certain knowledge of the world around us, whereas other fields, such as religion and philosophy, endlessly debated and were caught in interminable quarrels. But not science.

Why not take the method which was present in science and apply this method to everything? Why not apply it to religion? What not apply it to science?

First of all, what really was the method which science employed, rendering it so successful? Could the method be imitated? First find the method and then apply it to religion and theology and philosophy and law. Make sciences out of these fields also. Make every field into a science and every field will make progress in our knowledge of nature, just as science has. Make every field into a science and, just like science itself, every field will give us definite answers to all of our questions.

The method of science seemed to the men of The Age of Reason to consist of painstaking scrutiny and experiment into the secrets of Nature itself; the method of Reason itself. Hence, The Age of Reason.

As Kant claimed in the Preface to the Critique of Pure Reason, everything — all fields had to submit to the tribunal or the bar of reason, and nothing was exempt — not even religion. And philosophy had to submit to the trial of reason. Could it pass the test?

Kant thought that it could. He thought he would find a way to make philosophy a science once again just as it always had been when it reigned as queen of the sciences. Kant considered himself to be a product of the Age of Reason — a philosopher with a scientific mentality.

And indeed he was. He was talented in physics and mathematics; and, in some ways, he used these sciences as a model for his own philosophizing. But philosophy must be done in a new, scientific manner, the manner of the Age of Reason, which certainly affected all of Kant's philosophizing. The other external event which had an impact upon his philosophy was, as we have seen, the religious movement of Pietism.

The only way to be scientific about philosophy, in Kant's opinion, would be to subject reason itself to the judgment of the tribunal. What might this mean? Subject reason itself to trial. Could reason itself withstand its own trial? In other words, if we subject reason itself to the bar of reason, if we make an overview of reason itself, how will it fare?

Will reason itself be found to have limitations; and, if so, what are these limitations? What are the boundaries of reason itself? How much or how little might reason itself be able to tell us about reality? Is reason itself confined to occurrences or phenomena in space and time? Does the science of Kant's time, the science of Isaac Newton with his three laws of motion and his law of gravity, define the limits of everything that we can know speculatively? Kant appeared to think so for he responded strongly to the science of his time. But what lies beyond the boundaries of reason? The realm of faith? The realm of Kant's Pietism?

Speculative reason and science seemed to many in the Age of Reason to reveal that man was basically a machine and so not free. But Kant's Pietistic faith seemed to indicate that man had free choice; otherwise, morality would make no sense. Faith or reason? Science or religion? The science of The Age of Reason or his Pietistic faith? Kant had to choose between them, and he chose not one or the other but both. Speculative Reason and science dealt with the phenomenal realm of things-as-they-appear to us; faith dealt with the noumenal realm of things-in-themselves.

1. Scientific Discoveries

In the eighteenth century Age of Reason, it became increasingly obvious to many that the way to determine whether or not the earth was round was not to invent and multiply theories concerning a round or a flat earth but to try to sail around it. If your big experiment succeeded the way Magellan's experiment of this kind actually did succeed in the sixteenth century, then the earth actually was round and you proved your point.

Or consider the question as to how blood circulated in the human body. Might opening a cadaver help in answering this question? Vesalius, in the Italian Renaissance, was the first to perform this experiment; and he effectively demonstrated his point about the circulation of the blood.

This was the experimental method of discovering the truth. Why could not this method, so sure and so effective, become the new method of discovering the truth about everything. Simply observe and reason.

So thought the intellectuals, the philosophes of the European Enlightenment, The Age of Reason, and Kant asked himself the question — Are they perhaps right?

2. The Philosophes

The so-called philosophes, mostly French, flowered in the decades just before the French Revolution. As products of the eighteenth century world, they believed that science could do everything, including bringing man to a state of perfection on earth. Science would eventually cure disease and poverty and so bring about an earthly paradise. Becker refers to this as "The Heavenly City of the Eighteenth Century Philosophers", and he even wrote a book bearing that title.

This small circle included such names as Voltaire, Diderot d'Alembert and de Holbach. Diderot and d'Alembert collaborated in creating an Encyclopedia of all existing knowledge on any subject in the eighteenth century. De Holbach wrote a book entitled Man, the Machine, in which he likened man to a statue; only man takes in information from eyes and ears and nose and processes it just the way a machine would. Man, the Machine constituted the worldview of science on man. Was it correct? To what extent? Or did this worldview belong only to the realm of phenomena or of things-as-they-appear to us (Dinge-fur-uns) and not to noumena or of things-in-themselves (Dinge-an-sich). It was questions like this which Kant pondered.

3. Reaction to Religion

The men of the Enlightenment circle, by and large, did not trust the realm of faith. This is not to say that they denied the existence of God or even of morality. But they did not trust anything which they could not prove through reason; for example, the Bible. The Bible was a matter of revelation and of faith, not of reason. Most of the philosophes, with the notable exception of Rousseau, if we can truly place him in the Age of Reason, thought that man was determined, not free. Again, if this is so, how can we make sense out of morality? The philosophes definitely created here what amounted to a problem for Kant and his religious Pietism. Pietism was a religion based upon morality and experience, yes, but also upon the Christ of the New Testament Bible. Could Kant really have it both ways? He was attracted to the thinking of the Enlightenment but also to religious Pietism.

But how could he reconcile both? Could man really be both free and determined?

C. Kant's Synthesis

For Kant, man was both free and determined; free, as we have seen, in the noumenal realm of things-in-themselves, and determined in the phenomenal realm of things-as-they-appear-to-us, the realm of science. For Kant, both science and Pietism, his religion of morality are true; science in the phenomenal realm of things-for-us (Dinge-fur-uns), and religion and morality, along with GOD, FREEDOM, AND IMMORTALITY in the noumenal realm or in the realm of things as they really are, the realm of things-in-themselves (Dinge-an-sich).

In this way, Kant could have both his Enlightenment and his Pietistic background. In this way, Kant could have both science and religion. This has been the story of how one philosopher, a watershed figure in the history of philosophy, made a philosophic synthesis out of dualistically opposed movements in his life and times.

What is true of Kant is also true of Hegal who will constitute the next chapter in our continuing story of philosophers and the impact of their lives upon their respective philosophies.

FIVE PHILOSOPHERS

[1]Immanuel Kant, Preface to the Second Edition. Critique of Pure Reason, pp.xxx-xxxii. Preface to Prolegomena, p.2.

[2]Immanuel Kant, op.cit., pp.xxxi-xxxiii.

[3]Immanuel Kant, op.cit., p.xxxvii.

[4]Immanuel Kant, op.cit., pp. xxxii-xxxiv.

[5]Immanuel Kant, op.cit., p. xxxix.

[6]Allen W. Wood, Kant's Moral Religion, pp. 160-176.

[7]Allen W. Wood, op.cit., pp. 201-204.

[8]Ernst Cassirer, Kant's Life and Thought, pp. 16-18.

[9]Immanuel Kant, Religion Within the Limits of Reason Alone. Transl. with an Introduction by Theodore Greene. Intro. pp xii-xiv.

[10]Isaiah Berlin, The Age of Enlightenment, "Introduction", pp.14-29.

[11]Immanuel Kant, Critique of Pure Reason, "Preface", p. xxiv.

CHAPTER THREE

GEORGE WILHELM FRIEDRICH HEGEL:
THE SURROUNDING POLITICAL WORLD

The world into which Hegel was born was a world caught in the throes of revolution and change. It was the world of the French Revolution and of Napoleon Bonaparte. After Bonaparte, Europe would never be the same again despite a momentary reaction under Metternich. The ancien regime, the ancien aristocracy would never be as powerful in the future as it had been in the past. The culture of most of Europe would change; no longer would European literature be under the sway of Classicism; Romanticism became the style under Wordsworth and Coleridge and, in music, under Beethoven. In the world of popular culture, the waltz, a newer, freer style of dancing, replaced the minuet.

Everywhere, the concept of Romantic Revolution was in the air.[1] France was no longer a monarchy; now it was a Republic. Napoleon had conquered most of Europe; all of these conquered territories now wanted their independence and a nationalistic movement began throughout Europe. The Spanish, the Germans, the Italians all began to crave their independence.

At the time, much of central Europe was divided into three hundred or so principalities and a similar situation prevailed in southern Europe. All these territories began to look forward to the day when there would be a united Italy or a united Germany, depending on whether one was located in a principality in either southern or central Europe.

There were many currents of thought which were exerting their influence in the early nineteenth century: Romanticism, Nationalism, the French Revolution. Hegel was very much in touch with all of these movements and all of these movements had bearing on his philosophy. Of all philosophers, Hegel seems to have been the most conscious of the historical forces shaping his own time. At heart, he was an historian of the past and of the present.

Hegel's historical bend revealed itself early in life. When still in the Gymnasium, roughly equivalent to our high school system, Hegel would alphabetize items and arrange an encyclopedia of subjects for himself giving the history of each particular subject. Later in life, a sense of history would always be central to his philosophy.

His Phenomenology of Mind, published in 1807, was a landmark in the history of philosophy. In this work, Hegel traces the development of the mind from its earliest stages into its maturity. The internal history of the mind is described, from its beginnings in "Subjective Consciousness" through its movement to "Objective

Consciousness" and, finally, to its culmination in the maturity of "Absolute Consciousness". The stage of "Absolute Consciousness" most effectively reveals a synthesis, a combination of the best elements present in the two previous stages.

The first stage, "Objective Consciousness", represses pure inwardness or subjectivity. This stage depicts the inner psychology of the mind.[2] The second stage, "Self-Consciousness", could be described as the ethical or political stage in which the mind now strives to implement its ideas in the external world. The family, the church, and the State become the central units in this world.[3] The last stage, the third, is represented by "Free Concrete Mind". The mind finds expression in the highest forms of consciousness, art, religion, and philosophy. "Free Concrete Mind", "Absolute Mind" is a synthesis of the two previous stages. It combines the consciousness of the first stage with the self-consciousness of the second stage.[4]

For Hegel, the stage of "Free Concrete Mind" was also the expression of true individualism. It was the state in which the individual combined his subjectivity with the objective, external world of society, and in which both subjectivity and objectivity existed in harmony.

True individualism was not, for Hegel, the individual of the French Revolution, which manifested itself in "negative freedom", the sheer and simple freedom to do whatever one wanted, as Hegel saw it, pure anarchy. Like many of his contemporaries, he witnessed the culmination of the ideals of freedom of the French Revolution in the guillotine and the Reign of Terror. Pure subjectivity or "negative freedom" could not be the ideal of freedom.[5]

As he stressed later in The Philosophy of Right, published in 1821, the last of his published works during his life, "positive freedom", in which the subjective individual expresses himself in the objective, external world is actually the ideal of freedom for man. The Philosophy of Right traces the history of objective, subjective and Absolute Freedom.

This is also something which Hegel attempts in his Philosophy of History. In the first stage, the Oriental World of the despot ruling over a vast region, only One is Free. Later, in the Greco-Roman world of freemen and slaves, Some are Free. But, in the last stage of the Protestant, German world of northern Europe, All are Free. This scheme may or may not correspond to what actually takes place in all these epochs, but it is how Hegel viewed history — the march of Freedom through the world or, in Hegel's own words, "the march of God through the world".

In Hegel's conception, history was the unfolding of the dialectic of freedom. History moved forward by the clash of opposing forces — and the best elements in each force became combined in a new synthesis. History was involved with change or Becoming. "Becoming" was, in Hegel's view, reality.

This is the metaphysics of reality in general with Hegel elaborates in The Encyclopedia of the Philosophical Sciences. "Becoming" is the only reality for, if we think of the concept of "Being", this is simply the widest of all possible classes or classifications. The broadest possible class which we can think of contains no content whatsoever. The broadest possible class becomes immediately identical with "Nothing".

Hence, "Being" is "Nothing" or "Being is non-Being and reality, in this way, contradicts itself. Hegel's Logic and, indeed, his entire philosophy, is based upon the concept of Contradiction. The Law of non-Contradiction, in the metaphysics of the Schoolmen, was plainly not true for Hegel.

Being, or reality, to the contrary, was always contradicting itself. This was the essence of "Becoming" or the movement of "Being" to wider and wider and finally the widest of all possible concepts, "Nothing" or "Non-Being". The nature of mediation in Hegelian philosophy is that of moving from one stage to another dialectically and combining the best of previous stages.

Reality was "Becoming"; it was not a static entity; it was a dynamic force; it was, in today's terminology, a process. Reality was a process and Hegel is often classified, in the history of philosophy, as a Process Philosopher. A process Philosopher is one who thinks that the fundamental reality of the universe is change, that the universe does not consist of a collection of independent entities or things which do not change. Rather, it is a series of interconnected points which are constantly changing. The only constant is change itself, a point of view very much in line with today's thinking in which the only constant we witness is change itself.

Change itself is reality for Hegel; Becoming. In the ancient Greek world, it was the philosopher, Heraclitus, who held that reality was essentially Becoming — eternal fire, like the intake and the outtake of eternal flame.[6] And, in Hegel's philosophy, reality was Becoming, the clash of opposing forces propelling history forward in a dialectical process.

This was the march of the Absolute Mind (a spirit that may have been independent of the world, a Spirit that may constitute the mind of God) through the world. The foundation of this process was Spirit or Mind; hence, Dialectical Idealism.

One very prominent disciple of Hegel, Karl Marx (1818-1883), also viewed reality and, especially history, as a result of the clash between opposing forces; i.e., as a process, as a dialectical process. For this reason, Marx and the Marxists philosophers of many different persuasions are usually classified as Process Philosophers, along with Hegel, as well as along with several very contemporary Process Philosophers such as Hartshorne, Hocking and Brightmann.

However, neither Marx nor any of the Marxists really appear to have viewed Absolute Mind as the foundation of this process. Rather, they have viewed history as the strife of material forces which underly all of reality. This will be treated in more detail in the chapter dealing with Immanuel Mounier. For Marxists, Matter, rather than Absolute Mind, is at the foundation of reality. Hence, the Marxists, although dialectical in holding that reality is a Process, are not Dialectical Idealists but, rather, Dialectical Materialists. History for them is a process of one group after another trying to control the very material, economic "means of production". History is strife with struggle and process, but material process and not a process in the development of some Absolute Spirit.

In these major works which have been mentioned, Hegel slowly expounded his process view of reality. After his death in 1831, his pupils published his lectures from their own notes, which lectures were really explications of Hegel's dialectical, process view of reality in several areas such as the philosophy of religion, the philosophy and the history of philosophy.

Did the French Revolution really affect Hegel's philosophy of either his metaphysics or his ethics or both? Did the fate of a divided Germany or of Napoleon's conquests really affect Hegel's dialectical, process view of the world? In the following sections, I hope to show that these events did affect Hegel's worldview and that, like any sane individual, he responded to the historical currents with surrounded him.

A. France in Revolution

The ten-year revolution in France, 1789-1799, including the Reign of Terror, was a momentous event for all of Hegel's contemporaries. Hegel's predecessors, Fichte and Schelling, witnessed the birth, the momentous force, and the outcoming of this Revolution. So did Romantic poets in Germany such as Tieck and Novalis and Schiller and Holderlin. In England, Coleridge, Blake, and Wordsworth were well aware of what was taking place in France. The eyes of the entire world were very much upon that center of European culture, France. France was now a republic. It had beheaded its king and queen and the rest of the world stood in awe. If France was now a republic, why could not the Revolution now be extended throughout Europe. The aristocracy in every country was extremely afraid.

The immediate cause of the Revolution on France was the peasant crop failure of 1787. Starving peasants insisted upon land reform and they were later aided and abetted by the Third Estate or the bourgeoisie, who also desired land reform from the largely hereditary, landed aristocrat.

As a result of all these troubles, an angry mob stormed a government bastion of no particular significance, known as the Bastille. They liberated simply a few lunatics or alleged lunatics and prisoners. Nevertheless, this event in July of 1789 was symbolic of the beginning of the French Revolution and the French celebrated its two hundredth anniversary very recently.

The storming of the Bastille, however, did not end the nation's economic troubles; and, eventually, the Revolution fell into the hands of the most radical of political elements, the Jacobins. One of the most fanatical among them, Robespierre, guarded the gains of the Revolution with single-minded vigilance. France must not slide back into the hands of the aristocracy so it must ruthlessly guillotine all of its enemies and/or imagined enemies. In the Reign of Terror, all suspects were summarily guillotined; and there were often many executions during a given day.

In the end, many were dissatisfied with the blood and havoc Robespierre wreaked upon the populace, and so he was deposed and beheaded in turn. France was then headed by a temporary tribunal until one of its members overshadowed the tribunal. This was Napoleon who promised to reconcile the ancien regime, or aristocracy, with the new order of things. He also promised to liberate Europe but instead plunged it into ten years of bloody war from which everyone emerged tired and hoping for something better.

1. France and the Enlightenment

The immediate cause of the French Revolution may have been the wheat crop failure, but there were also more remote causes. The writings of Rousseau and Voltaire and d'Alembert and Diderot in the small intellectual circle of French philosophes may have to be numbered among those more remote causes.

The philosophes of the Age of Enlightenment, alluded to previously, laid the theoretical foundation for the right of any people to rebel against the sovereign. Many of them, especially Rousseau, relied upon the myth of the "social contract". The "Social Contract" is the title of what is probably Rousseau's major political work.

Although the origins of the "social contract" are probably mythical, as Rousseau himself admits, the contract serves a useful function. It is an attempt at explaining the purpose of good government. The "social contract" could also be employed to explain the function of ideal government. Good government, in the mind of the philosophe of the Enlightenment, also had to submit to what Kant called the tribunal or the bar of reason.

What was the reason government existed at all? Was there any real reason for all of the artificiality which surrounded the court of the aristocracy in the eighteenth century France? Was this a natural government, philosophes such as Rousseau asked themselves.

They answered that any government was natural if it serves the natural ends of government; i.e., if it served the ends for which government existed in the minds of its citizens, namely, promotion of the well being of its subjects. For this reason and this reason only, did the sovereign, whoever the sovereign or group of people might be, have the natural right to rule at all in the first place. Good government, then, was supposed to rest upon an implicit agreement or contract between the ruler or sovereign and the subjects.

The essence of the unwritten, tacit contract was that the subjects would agree to obey the law and be ruled if, and only if, the sovereign authority would fulfill its end of the bargain and promote the natural good of its subjects with justice and equality.

According to this theory of the origin of government, the theory of Rousseau and also of many of the philosophes, the rights of the sovereign were conditioned upon the consent of the subjects and could be abrogated if, for example, the sovereign did not rule for the people's benefit and did not promote justices and liberty and equality. Then, according to Rousseau and many others in this tradition, the subject had a right to rebellion against the sovereign.

One can readily see the individualism upon which such a theory rests. The contract is a philosophic agreement among individuals in order to accomplish a specific purpose. This was the reason government arose and not out of a primary social need, at least as far as the philosophes were concerned.

It is this same sense of individualism in the philosophes of the Enlightenment which, along with the more immediate wheat crisis, inspired the French Revolution. Here, the sovereign monarch and aristocracy, in the minds of its people, were no longer fulfilling their function of promoting justices or freedom or equality in land reform and should, therefore, be rebelled against.

2. Liberty, Equality, and Fraternity

But the Revolution culminated in the guillotine of the Reign of Terror as we have already seen. It also culminated in ten years of civil war in Europe under Napoleon as we have also seen. And all of this was the result of freedom and individualism.

Or at least this was the way Hegel viewed the situation. Like many of his contemporaries, he at first supported the cause of the French Revolution with heartfelt enthusiasm. But when he saw the guillotine, which may have been its logical culmination, he reacted with horror. What went wrong? Could the concept of freedom itself possibly be wrong?

Consider, also, Napoleon and the wars of conquest. Napoleon also was an important outcome of the French Revolution yet he was a dictator now causing the suffering of Europe. Perhaps, Hegel reasoned, it was not the consent of Freedom itself which was at fault but only a certain type of Freedom. Perhaps it was what he called the mindlessness of the "negative freedom" of the French Revolution, which prides itself on its thoroughgoing individualism.

This freedom is reckless and adolescent; it consists entirely of a "freedom from" something but contains no notion of a "freedom for" something constructive in society. Therefore, the need for a positive freedom, the need for the sense of a freedom for something, integration with or development in the political and ethical life of the society. Or perhaps, integration with and development in the art, religion, and philosophe of a given society; i.e., the Absolute Mind in Hegel's philosophy, once again.

Here again, the philosopher, Hegel, responded in his environment like a truly intelligent human being. The concept of negative freedom may be said to have truly arisen from the Revolution itself, and the concept of positive freedom to have arisen from a lack in the environment; i.e., the need for a concept of freedom which was tied to order and stability and, most important of all, human development.

B. Division of the German World

Now, again, the German world of Hegel culminated in a deeply divided world. In the literature of the late nineteenth century, there is a sense of pride in the Volkgeist of the folk spirit of the German people. But there was no unified nation to match it, much like the division of Germany today under the Berlin Wall, only worse.

1. The Three Hundred Divisions

Central Europe, in Hegel's time, consisted of hundreds of petty, warring principalities, each striving to be dominant over its neighbors. This was the result of the bitter Thirty Years War over religion which devastated one-third the population of Germany in the seventeenth century. Everyone wanted a united Germany but how to achieve it?

Political reunification was finally achieved under Bismarck in 1870 with Prussia leading the way. But this was well after Hegel's time. Hegel had already died in 1831, and so he never lived to see the political unification of all of Germany, which he and many of his contemporaries dreamed about and longed for.

2. Fichte's Nationalism

In 1814, the philosopher, Johann Gottlieb Fichte, one of Hegel's famous predecessors in German philosophy, wrote his famous tract, Addresses to the German Nation. It was a patriotic call to all Germans, the creators of a great culture, to work toward the unification of Germany. The addresses affected all of Fichte's contemporaries and the affected Hegel. Hegel's philosophy, among many other things which it certainly is, is a philosophy of unification

C. Hegel's Solution

Hegel's philosophy, even the metaphysics, is by and large a political philosophy. This is well known; it is a truism. The concepts of negative and positive freedom, the concepts of alienation, of the individual, the family, the state are all political realities, which political realities represent the external world, in Hegel's thought. Hegel was simply an intelligent human being, a genius responding to the needs of his time.

There was a real need in the external environment of Hegel's century for a concept of positive freedom; for a real harmony between the individual and society which would allow for real human growth and development. Hegel existed in the world of the French Revolution. In the beginning, he accepted all of the goals and ideals of that world. But as time went on, this became impossible for him. Like many others of his generation, he experienced the culmination of that Revolution, with all of its stated goals for the freedom of man, in an extremely tyrannical Reign of Terror. Many in the aristocracy lost their heads and the rights of the individual were plainly trampled upon. How could this form of freedom constitute a legitimate goal for man? It was plain that it could not.

Hegel had to cast around for an alternative to the negative freedom of the Revolution, for it had plainly enough discredited itself. Where could he find the alternative? Again, only in a concept of positive freedom, in which the individual could find his true home in the community; in which the alienation between the individual and the community could be overcome. The purpose of Hegel's entire philosophy was to express this new sense of individualism — in which the individual felt his individuality expressed in the community — in short, in the concept of what Hegel called "positive freedom".

[1]Charles Taylor, Hegel, p.3 and the entire first chapter, "Aims of a New Epoch", pp.3-50.

[2]G.W.F. Hegel, The Phenomenology of Mind, "A. Consciousness", pp.147-213.

[3]G.W.F. Hegel, op. cit., "B. Self-Consciousness", pp.215-267.

[4]G.W.F. Hegel, op. cit., "C. Free Concrete Mind", pp.269-808.

[5]G.W.F. Hegel, op cit.., pp.265-267.

[6]G. S. Kirk and J. E. Raven, The Presocratic Philosophers, pp. 199-202, Ch.6, #7.

CHAPTER FOUR

JOHN DEWEY AND THE TWENTIETH CENTURY

John Dewey (1859-1952) was born and raised in the United States, and he spent many years teaching in the University of Columbia and in the University of Chicago. He is an extremely important figure in American philosophy and in world philosophy. Fifty years after his death, he is well remembered today.

In the twentieth century, according to John Dewey, philosophy sorely needed to be restructured or overhauled. This was the title of his well-known work, Reconstruction in Philosophy, written in 1920.[1] He states in this work that philosophy has to abandon the concept of absolute or of fixed and unchanging truths. Truth, quite to the contrary, is always changing and must always be adapted to different problems. For example, a man struggling to get out of the woods does not determine on one theory of the correct path to follow out of the woods, if that path does not really succeed in getting him out of the woods. Rather, he constantly keeps changing his plans until he adopts a plan that is successful. The successful plan is the plan which will enable him to get out of the woods. This is the only true plan and all the other plans are plainly false.

Truth, for Dewey, the pragmatist, is judged by its consequences. Ideas, for Dewey, are merely instruments which enable us to find the correct solution to our problems. We must abandon the old habit of thinking of them as fixed entities unto themselves.

Our Reconstruction in Philosophy must replace the notion of fixed entities or of absolutes with the notion of relative truth. Truth is relative to the situation.

The same is true of morality, Dewey informs us, in his work of 1922, Human Nature and Conduct.[2] We cannot say that morals ought to be social for morals are social. Morals are relative to the end of action and in no sense Absolute.

In the area of education, Dewey was also a pioneer for here, also, he applied his instrumentalist philosophy. Ideas are instruments and one learns by actually employing one's ideas. One is not a spectator in real learning but, rather, one learns by doing. We should be participants in the act of learning.

One learns to write by actually writing. One learns to walk by actually walking and to speak by actually speaking. In a similar vein, one might say that we learn anything not by simply being passive and listening, but by actually engaging with the speaker in dialogue. This is the well-known Socratic method of teaching and of learning, and it is a favorite example of what later disciples of Dewey meant by this method of education. Also, engaging in projects, research, etc.

In reality, Dewey did set philosophy on a completely new footing. It would never be the same again. Many contemporary philosophers now realize that philosophy must be practical and that it must be rooted in the social world. For many, the "Reconstruction in Philosophy" has already begun.

Dewey lived in a world which was a product of two new outlooks upon the world: the outlook of modern science and the outlook of modern democratic politics. Both modes of thought were embedded in his philosophy; i.e., both in his practical proposals and in his general worldview. How both of these attitudes in twentieth century thought entered into Dewey's philosophizing is the story we are now about to tell.

A. The Scientific Temper

Science was now much more than a method of thought, which it had been in much of Renaissance philosophy and in The Age of Reason or the Enlightenment, which we have previously encountered. It was now a technological reality. Through the use of the fruits of science, man was able to solve many of his specific, practical problems and better his standard of living. In Dewey's time, science had brought about the jet, the airplane, the automobile, and improved methods of transportation in general; also, the invention of skyscrapers and central heating. In short, most inventions were in heavy commercial use in Dewey's time except for the computer.

1. The Triumph of Science

In Dewey's mind, nothing could account for the triumph of science except slow, painstaking investigation and trial-and-error. Science would approach a given problem first from one angle, then from another. The only thing which mattered for science was the result; which method worked. The method which worked was the true one. All of this was very much in line with Dewey's pragmatism.

He agreed with the scientific, pragmatic approach in philosophy, which defined truth as the ideal limit of inquiry, upon which all investigation converged. This was the method whereby the individual reached truth in daily life. The individual would attempt one method, then another. The method which worked was the true method. It was that method which would enable the individual to find his way out of the woods.

The pragmatic method, the method upon which all research would converge in the end, according to C. S. Peirce (and Dewey agreed with Peirce), was the method of science and also of daily life. It was the true method of problem-solving. The theory which is true solves our problem. If the pragmatic method actually worked this well in science and in ordinary life, Dewey thought that the same method might also be employed in philosophy as well.

Philosophy should be experimental. It should treat ideas as instruments for solving problems. For ideas were not things-in-themselves as some philosophers seemed to think. Ideas should be regarded both from the standpoint of their usefulness in practical problem-solving and also from the standpoint of their contribution to the ideal convergence of ideas in research. What worked for science (and also daily life) should work for philosophy. This was simply another of many tries, to varying degrees successful, to put philosophy on a scientific footing.

The enormous success story of science in the social world surrounding him has a great impact upon the thinking of John Dewey.

2. The Problem with Philosophy

Dewey's problem matched Kant's in several respects. Both men thought that science was always making progress, whereas philosophy was constantly dealing with the same old problems and never finally solving them. Philosophy is still asking "What is the moral good?" and "What is Reality?" without ever answering these questions once and for all in a manner such that no one could ever dispute the answers. Once again, both men looked upon science as more sure-footed; it seemed to have the ideal method for solving problems, whereas philosophy did not share the same method.

Could one find out what this method was, divorce it from science, and then apply it to philosophy? Whatever the method was, what worked for science should work for philosophy.

In Dewey's opinion, this method was basically a trial-and-error method, a method of using ideas as instruments in order to solve problems. One would be ready to abandon one's ideas the moment the ideas or concepts did not bear fruit; i.e., the moment the ideas or concepts did not solve problems. Successful ideas solved problems.[3]

If only ideas could be treated experimentally as instruments in philosophy, then philosophy would make progress. Then and only then could it take its rightful place among the sciences of the world. Instrumentalism, the philosophy that all ideas are instruments for solving problems, was the only workable philosophy. It was the reason science succeeded because it operated under a sound, correct philosophy.

3. Need for Reconstruction

It then became necessary to overhaul philosophy, to restructure it, at least as Dewey saw the problem. First, it became necessary to abandon the concept of the absolute and to replace it with the concept of the relative. Truth, for Dewey, was relative; it was a matter of solving problems. When an individual solved one problem, he worked on another; the scientific method for Dewey. The ultimate goal of research, the ultimate goal of practical living, no one knew. Some of Dewey's critics might well ask, at this point, then why take any practical steps in living if we do not know the ultimate goal? Where does it all converge?

Dewey appeared to have vague ideas of Progress and of the growth and development of civilization. Do these then constitute an absolute? If they do not, then do the ideas of Progress and growth and civilization all seem to lose some of their moral force? These are questions which cannot be answered in this essay but they are well worth consideration.

But for Dewey, philosophy plainly had to be restructured or, in his words, reconstructed. Ideas of absolute truth and absolute morality had to be reconstructed with concepts of relative truth and relative morality. The view of ideas as things-in-themselves had to be reconstructed with a view of ideas as instruments which will aid philosophers in solving their problems.

Dewey's ideas are accepted by many schools of thought today; maybe all of them would claim that their concepts enable them to solve problems. This is a tribute of Dewey's success; to a philosopher who responded to the triumph of science in the world around him.

B. Social Reform

But science was not the only external influence upon the mind of Dewey. In the social world, he also saw the necessity for progress. Dewey equated Progress with Democracy and longed for the extension of democratic politics throughout the world.

Democracy solved problems and worked toward Progress, he thought. In this respect, it was the same as science. It employed the scientific method of cooperative inquiry.

Dewey was not content with philosophy alone. In his many writings, he also viewed himself as a social reformer, helping to extend the democratic traditions he knew and the scientific method he knew, throughout the world.

1. Democracy's Extension

The First World War was fought, many thought at the time, to save the world for democracy. It was a popular slogan. The period between the two World Wars, however, witnessed the temporary triumph of non-democratic, totalitarian forms of government, especially of Communism and Fascism in many countries.

Could one, through propoganda, import our form of government throughout the rest of the world? Recently, this tactic seems to have enjoyed a great deal of success, both in South America (witness the fall from power of many dictators in their respective countries) and in Eastern Europe (the democratic reforms in East Germany, Poland, Hungary and Czechoslovakia).

So today, the question may very well be, could this method be extended throughout the rest of the world? In Dewey's time, however, the time of the First World War and its aftermath, the same question did not meet with an answer which was nearly as successful. Democracy's possible extension, if such it be, was temporarily slowed down.

Yet Dewey persisted with his initial optimism. He never lost his faith in democracy and science; these two movements, in his view, could be extended throughout the world.

2. Progress and Philosophy

Dewey's faith in philosophy followed through with this same ideal. Philosophy, by following the scientific method, paralleled democracy. It would, as reconstructed, and with an instrumentalist vision, help spread democracy throughout the world.

C. Education

We have mentioned how Dewey was not content with philosophy alone. He was the sort of man who wanted to see philosophy applied. One of the applied areas which interested him very much was the area of education.

1. Science and Democracy

Ideas were definitely related for John Dewey. If science and democracy were great harbingers of success, why should they not be employed in education? What should not education on all levels be scientific as well as democratic? What would the application of science and democracy to education mean?

2. The New Philosophy of Education

Science, democracy, and education; for Dewey, these three ideas were deeply intertwined. A democratic, scientific education was an education in which dialogue was not only permitted but encouraged; an education in which one learned by doing, by trying to solve problems by trial-and-error. This method alone insured Progress.

Both in his world view and in his theory of education, Dewey was a man both of and for the twentieth century. The scientific and democratic ideas of his time became a part of the man himself, and he expressed these currents of thought in his whole philosophy, in everything he wrote.

It is now time to examine the last philosopher on our list, Emmanuel Mounier. He also responded to many twentieth century currents of thought. But for Mounier, the major question of his time could be interpreted as the question, "What is a real democracy?".

[1]John Dewey, Reconstruction in Philosophy, New York, 1920.
[2]John Dewey, Human Nature and Conduct, New York, 1922.
[3]Morton White, The Age of Analysis, p.55.

CHAPTER FIVE

EMMANUEL MOUNIER: COMMUNISM AND CAPITALISM

Communism or Capitalism: Which system is better? Is it possible today to even ask such a question? One might claim that Communism has obviously failed and that the proof, if one needs it, is in Eastern Europe. But can we even compare these systems in the abstract? As pure, abstract forms, both of these systems seem to have failed. The future may belong to a combination of the two; i.e., some free enterprise along with some bureaucracy or state planning.

At any rate, in comparing both of these, are we guilty of a category mistake, not too much unlike that of comparing apples with oranges? And if so, to what extent? Capitalism relates to an economic system, whereas Communism is a political system of Totalitarianism. Or at least so some might claim.

But there are others who will maintain that Communism is an economic system and employ the term in its old-fashioned sense, according to the slogan of Marx's Critique of the Gotha Program, "From each according to his ability, to each according to his need".

Politically, one might say that there are two broad categories of government; governments are either Democratic or Totalitarian or somewhere in between. Economically, there are two basic ways of running the economy: Capitalism or Communism or somewhere in between.

So there are many possible arrangements. One could be a Capitalist economically and a Totalitarian Dictator politically; witness the example of the recently deposed Pinochet in Chile. Or, on the other hand, an entire nation could be Capitalistic economically and politically democratic, as is true of the United States and the European democracies.

Two other combinations are possible. Communism (or Socialism), in the U.S.S.R. before Gorbachev was not democratic politically. But now, under Gorbachev, it may turn Democratic politically while remaining economically Socialist. At least, these appear to be Gorbachev's plans.

What has this to do with Emmanuel Mounier? It is the point of this chapter to show how the philosophy of Mounier came to grips with the problems of Capitalism and Communism, even if category mistakes can be involved here. Is it possible to combine the best of the economic systems of both Capitalism and Communism with a humane, Democratic political system? Mounier apparently thought so, and why he thought so is our story in this last chapter.

Mounier thought that both could be combined in a philosophy which avoided the extremes of Totalitarian socialism on the one hand, or with cut-throat Capitalistic competition on the other. This was the philosophy of Personalism, which placed the human person at the center of all values. It was a philosophy which resembled Existentialism in many respects.

For Mounier, in the philosophy of Personalism, personal relationships were the goal of life; and they were more important than the conquest of nature or than making money. In many senses, all political and economic philosophies had to square with Personalism; did they make the individual Person the center of all reality? If so, they were correct philosophies.

But Communist Totalitarianism did not make the Person the center of all values; it ruthlessly suppressed dissent and did not allow for individual rights. But Capitalism did not make the Person the center of all values either; its competitive values had plainly sold out to crass commercialism.

How could one really be a Personalist and go in between? Mounier's lifework was a campaign to do just this; and, hence, his Personalist philosophy tries to balance the external forces of Communist Totalitarianism and unrestrained Capitalism. And now to the story of how Mounier tries to accomplish just this through his Personalist philosophy.

A. Communist Environment

Emmanuel Mounier (1905-1950) lived a life which was tragically short. He died at the age of forty-five. His life span between the two World Wars, although Mounier lived in France and Dewey in America, was similar in one respect. It resembled what Charles Dickens has called the best and worst of times.

Both men certainly lived in exciting times when Totalitarian forms of government, both Communist and Fascist, vied for world attention and world acceptance of their respective ideologies. Many more in the intellectual world seemed to lean toward Communism than toward Fascism.

Would Communism capture the imagination of men everywhere? If so, was their any possibility it would ever shed its bureaucratic, Totalitarian, high-handed manner? Most thought that this was plainly impossible and they may very well have been right.

For most, Communism was the symbol of anti-democracy and they feared for the future of democracy itself. For despite the rivalry between Fascism and Communism, the presence of both seemed to presage the dwindling of Democracy.

In Mounier's philosophy of Personalism, Democracy was considered to be very important for the preservation and growth of the individual. But it had to be true Democracy. Did capitalism always favor the true development of the individual in a human direction? It seemed plain to Mounier that this was frequently not the case. Capitalism encouraged competition at the expense of all other values. Competition could be cut-throat; hence, not a genuine human value.

Since Personalism placed human values at the center of reality, Capitalism could not qualify, any more than Communism, as the standard-bearer of human values. The true philosophy of Personalism could embrace neither current so-called democracies with their capitalism nor their opposition in the new, mutually rivaling factions of Fascism and Communism. For Mounier, neither the capitalism of the European countries nor the Communism of Russia promoted genuine human values, values in accordance with the philosophy of Personalism.[1]

1. Communist Theoreticians

The intellectual, political world in which Mounier lived was dominated by Marx, Lenin, Trotsky, and Stalin; by revisionists on the left, such as Trotsky and Deborin, and by revisionists on the right, such as Eduard Bernstein and Plekhanov. Political leaders such as Lenin, and later Stalin, held fast to the center.[2]

But there were many deviationists to either extreme, left or right. To the right, Eduard Bernstein in Germany initiated the Social Democratic party, holding to the belief that Socialism could come about peacefully, without revolution, through free, parliamentary democratic elections. To the left, men like Trotsky urged peasant uprisings and worldwide revolution. In the center, Lenin, and especially Stalin, wanted to build socialism in one country, Russia. Stalin brutally executed all of his opposition and led his country into a dictatorship.

The cruelty of a Stalinist dictatorship represented everything Mounier found cruel and inhuman in Communism. But he could sympathize with the sentiments of a Bernstein and with all those people everywhere who would hold to a truly democratic form of socialism. Not that democratic socialism is a necessary consequence of Personalism, which dictated no one political philosophy. But Personalism would rule out all those philosophies which evidently were not human.

2. Communism as a World Power

In Mounier's time, the Communist ideology embraced only one country, Russia. Around the time of Mounier's death, it also seized power in China. Early socialism and/or Communism claimed the goal of world domination. Everywhere, the worker must be at least a part owner of the means of production through which he earned his livelihood. This amounts to the old definition of Socialism, which is in dispute today. Does one really have to hold to abolition of private property in the means of production in order to be a Socialist today? Many will claim not so.

But the largest political question for Mounier's time was the question, "Will Communism one day dominate the entire world with its political ideology?".

3. Communism and Totalitarianism

The second largest question for Mounier and others was whether wither Communism or Socialism could be divorced from Totalitarianism, the total concentration of power in the hands of one or a few people, with its attendant abrogation of human rights. Were Personalism and Socialism compatible? Mounier thought they were; but disciples of his own Personalist philosophy, and also others who thought these values were compatible.

B. Capitalist Environment

The Capitalist world of Europe and America had its problems. This was the era of the Great Depression, and the Communist world was eager to seize upon it as an excellent example of the shortcomings of Capitalism in relying upon the unpredictability of private investment in the means of production, the stock market in short.

1. Philosophers of Capitalism

Adam Smith in The Wealth of Nations had two hundred years ago revealed how private vices like greed can be a public virtue, in the sense of making the entire commonwealth a little more affluent. This was like de Mandeville's Fable of the Bees, or Private Vices, Public Virtues. The industrious, selfish, greedy bees, by gathering honey for their own nest, actually contribute to the plenitude and richness of honey in the entire hive. By helping their greedy selves, they help everyone.

According to Adam Smith and others, the same was true of Capitalism. By encouraging selfish greed, it actually encouraged virtues such as industry and also contributed to growth and development and the wealth of the entire nation.

But, according to Mounier, Capitalism could also be quite inhuman. It could encourage cut-throat competition at the expense of almost everyone, except the few who profited from it, the entrepreneurs.

2. The Capitalist World

The Capitalist world embraced both Europe and America. Like Communism, the question between the wars was whether the European and the American way of life would export its Capitalist ideology and philosophy throughout the rest of the world or whether Capitalism was really in decline? Mounier actually thought that both Capitalism and Communism would soon dwindle as world influences for the reason that neither adequately squared with genuine humanistic or Personalist values.

3. Inhumanity of Capitalism

Does cut-throat competition with its attendant unemployment truly represent the highest values of man? Not according to Mounier. Imagine what he would have thought of our current situation of unemployment with so many homeless. But if Capitalism does not represent the highest values of the human, what is the correct opinion? If Mounier's opinions are correct, then what can we consider to be the true solution?

C. The Philosophy of Personalism

The only true answer for Mounier lies in the philosophy of Personalism, the human person as the only center of all values. Capitalism is greedy; Communism is ruthless. Neither ideology brings out the best in the human person. Mounier's times called, in his opinion, for a synthesis, the best in Capitalism with the best in

Communism.

1. Synthesis

Any true or human government, for Mounier, must respect the rights of man. It could not foster brutality and ruthlessness. It could not falsely imprison people. But neither could it constantly encourage ruthless competition and taking advantage of others. In other words, it must eliminate the worst features in both Capitalism and Communism. Then and only then will it arrive at a true synthesis, a truly human government.

It is interesting to note in all this how Mounier is almost totally immersed in his surrounding environment of the European world between two World Wars. Who would eventually dominate the world, Communists or Capitalists?

Mounier hoped neither of them would dominate the world for neither of them stood for truly human values, real kindness and concern for the human person.

2. Concrete Applications

The person was not the "abstract individual" of economic Capitalism. The true person was the concrete individual who was immersed in his environment and in the world of other people. He was not a cut-throat competitor; neither did he live under a brutal dictatorship. The experience of Mounier's life and the times in which he lived had taught him the necessity for a truly human philosophy which, in his opinion, must be a synthesis of the human values in both Capitalism and Communism.

[1]Emmanuel Mounier, _Personalism_.

[2]Gustav A. Wetter, _Dialectical Materialism_, esp. Chs. 6 and 10.

EPILOGUE

We have now completed our story. We have examined five philosophers: J. S. Mill, Kant, Hegel, Dewey, and Immanuel Mounier. We have looked at their problems and the sources of those problems in their lives and times. Their respective philosophies were, precisely, an attempt to deal with these problems. We have seen their respective dualisms and the divergent sources of these dualisms in their lives and times. Finally, we have all viewed their attempts at solving these problems, the respective syntheses between one tendency and another, which is often its opposite.

It appears that both from their own lives and also from the era of the surrounding world in which they find themselves located, all five of these philosophers managed to draw opposing tendencies together in one larger synthesis. In the case of J. S. Mill, it was the opposing tendencies of father and wife. In the example of Kant, it was the tension between a religious upbringing and the underlying scientific philosophies of the eighteenth century. For Hegel, it was the tension between freedom for the individual and the need for a united Germany. For Dewey, it was in putting together twentieth century science and democracy. And for Mounier, the problem of finding a third way between pure Capitalism and pure Communism.

Problems in their lives and times and an underlying final dualism seem to characterize all five of these philosophers. If this is true of five prominent philosophers in the history of Western thought, might it not be true of philosophy itself? In other words, by way of concluding reflections to this work, might it be the case that all philosophers enter philosophy in order to solve some pressing problem in their lives and/or times, which problem often pulls them mentally in opposite directions until they resolve their dilemma, often by synthesis? It is important to know that the surrounding world presents the problem and that the philosopher then often makes it his life's work to set himself/herself about to solving the pressing problem. Perhaps everyone who enters philosophy enters it for this reason.